Unlikely Conversations About Jesus

Six Dramas For Lent

Jon Joyce

CSS Publishing Company, Inc., Lima, Ohio

UNLIKELY CONERSATIONS ABOUT JESUS

Revised edition 1997

Second Printing 1976
Third Printing 1977

Library of Congress Cataloging-in-Publication Data

Joyce, Jon L.
Unlikely conversations about Jesus / Jon L. Joyce.
p. cm.
ISBN 0-89536-244-9 (pbk.)
1. Lent. 2. Drama in Christian education. 3. Drama in public worship. 4. Bible plays, American. I. Title.
BV85.J65 1997
246.'723—dc21 96-37175
CIP

ISBN: 0-89536-244-9 PRINTED IN U.S.A.

To the people of Holy Trinity Lutheran Church, Englewood, Ohio, who performed and endured the original versions of these mini-dramas.

Table Of Contents

Introduction 7

Synopsis 9

Production Notes 11

Suggested Program or Bulletin Announcements 13

1. An Elder And Peter Before The Passover 15

2. Judas And Mary Magdalene After The Last Supper 25

3. Caiaphas And Pilate's Wife Between The Trials 35

4. Simon Of Cyrene And Herod After The Trials 45

5. Joseph Of Arimathea And Barabbas During The Crucifixion 53

6. Pilate And Jesus' Mother After The Crucifixion 63

Introduction

Unlikely Conversations About Jesus is a series of six mini-dramas designed for the Lenten Season to help refresh the memory and experience of the people of God concerning the suffering and death of Jesus Christ — and the decision about him which he demands of each of us.

Unlikely Conversations use scriptural witness and Christian tradition to bring the Passion Story to life through imaginary conversations between real persons involved in that story. They are "unlikely" simply because it is not likely that these persons ever talked together, and it is less likely that they met and talked in the circumstances described in the mini-dramas.

These six portrayals of the Passion Story from a fresh perspective are further designed to give some insight into the character, feelings, and personal torture that many of those involved in it in Jerusalem may have experienced. In so doing, the mini-dramas portray the eternal turmoil, torture, and decision-making process which Jesus of Nazareth demands from each one of us.

These mini-dramas may be performed on stage or in a church chancel. Each in the series involves two persons in dialogue, with three of the mini-dramas also using a narrator. Required properties are minimal; costuming is versatile. The mini-dramas may be memorized or they may be bound and used in the "walking-reading" manner.

Synopsis

Unlikely Conversations About Jesus

1. An Elder And Peter Before The Passover

The emotional and exuberant disciple, Simon Peter, en route to secure a place for the disciples' Passover meal with Jesus, encounters a Jerusalem Elder. The Elder is both curious about Jesus and reluctant to reveal his feelings and the facts he knows to Peter.

2. Judas And Mary Magdalene After The Last Supper

Judas Iscariot, the disciple who betrayed Jesus, meets Mary Magdalene on a Jerusalem street, as he is rushing from the Upper Room to the High Priest's Palace to carry out the betrayal plot. Mary is alarmed at the rumors she has heard; Judas begins to feel the torture of what he has planned.

3. Caiaphas And Pilate's Wife Between The Trials

Claudia Procula, the wife of Pontius Pilate, pays a visit to Caiaphas, the High Priest who insisted upon Jesus' execution, in the latter's palace during the brief interval between Jesus' trial before the Sanhedrin and his trial before Pilate. Caiaphas is wary of her. Claudia is determined to stop her husband from sentencing the innocent carpenter to death.

4. Simon Of Cyrene And Herod After The Trials

Simon, the man who was to be forced, within hours, to carry Jesus' cross, stops in curiosity near Herod's Jerusalem residence when he sees the commotion that Jesus caused there. Soon the Tetrarch of Galilee comes out for a brief stroll, after the exertion of his mocking and scorning Jesus, and the two meet. Herod is indignant; Simon, appalled, moans at the thought of the execution and the unbearable weight of carrying a cross.

5. Joseph Of Arimathea And Barabbas During The Crucifixion

Joseph, a member of the Sanhedrin who voted for the execution of Jesus although secretly a follower of Jesus, stands side by side with Barabbas, the crude murderer who was freed from the death sentence when the crowd called for Jesus' death in his place, as the crucifixion commences in the distance.

6. Pilate And Jesus' Mother After The Crucifixion

The grief-stricken mother of Jesus visits Pilate in his throne room within hours of the crucifixion. Mary is, at first, beside herself with grief, and then composed and confident that she has not heard the last of her son. Pilate, weary and yet curious, is disturbed by her words, even though he wants to consider the whole matter closed.

Production Notes

These six mini-dramas are designed so that suggested settings, properties, and costumes may be used, along with sound effects in some instances. Or, they may be presented quite simply, using modern dress appropriate to each character, with no settings and minimal properties. When used in this latter way, the setting needs to be described in written or verbal form to help the audience "see" what is happening.

This series is also designed so that settings and costumes, if employed, may be economically used.

Settings

The setting for the buildings of a Jerusalem street on canvas (or cardboard) called for in #1 may be used again in #2 (with lighting set for night) and still again as a distant background in #4.

Costumes

Some of the suggested costumes may be used in several of the mini-dramas and may be varied by the use of different accessories.

The costume suggested for Simon Peter in #1 may also be used for Judas in #2; for Caiaphas in #3; perhaps for Herod in #4; and for Joseph in #5.

Mary Magdalene's costume in #2 may be worn (with adjustment so that it is white only) by Claudia Procula in #3.

The costume for the Elder in #1 is suitable for Simon of Cyrene in #4.

Rings, which may be borrowed from friends or from a friendly jeweler, may be used from week to week on different characters.

Sound Effects

Sound effects are indispensable in some of the mini-dramas. Sound effects may be obtained easily on sound effect records from a public library or by imaginative recording on tape specifically for these mini-dramas.

Sound effects called for include:

#1 — Marketplace noises. This should include people walking on dirt roads, talking, bargaining, with an occasional peddler yelling to sell his wares.

#3 — Crowing of a cock.

#4 — Noise of a large crowd. This could include cheering, booing, yelling, tumultuous sounds.

#5 — Noise of a large crowd. May repeat use of #4. Thunder, rain, lightning crackling. Imaginative use of splashing water, the crinkling of a paper bag or aluminum foil, and the crackling of light wood close to a sensitive microphone will suffice. Or, use a storm from a sound effects record.

Narrators

A narrator is used in three of the mini-dramas: #2, 4, and 5. The narrator ought to be unseen in each case, his voice strong enough to carry from backstage or from the rear of an auditorium. If possible, use a microphone and public address system for the narrator; this method is generally more effective.

Music

Musical selections, in the form of solos, are suggested for #4 and #6. Other musical selections, whether specifically performed or sung by the entire audience, should be carefully selected to fit the precise theme of each mini-drama.

Memorization

These mini-dramas will be most effective if each character memorizes his lines, gestures, and movements and rehearses them until he is at home in feeling his part.

However, it is also possible to present these sketches effectively if the characters use scripts in the "walking-reading" manner. In doing this, it is necessary that detailed study of the lines, gestures, and movements accompany thorough rehearsals so that the characters need only glance at the script while keeping gestures, movements, and eye contact with one another and the audience at maximum dramatic level.

Suggested Program Or Bulletin Announcements

In presenting these mini-dramas, it is important to state clearly, in writing or verbally, that the dramatic conversation about to be offered is imaginary — "unlikely" in that it did not occur, so far as we know.

It is suggested that, in a program or bulletin, each drama be listed in this way:

Unlikely Conversations About Jesus

1. An Elder And Peter Before The Passover

and so on, throughout the series.

The following note may be placed in a program or bulletin or read before each presentation:

> *Unlikely Conversations About Jesus* is a series of six mini-dramas presented to help refresh our memory and experience of the suffering and death of Jesus Christ. The most notable point about these conversations is that, so far as we know, they did not occur as we will present them, if at all. They are based on the scriptural witness, Christian tradition, and some dramatic imagination into the character which is portrayed. Each of the six "conversations" involves two persons from the Passion Story as it unfolded in Jerusalem, with several in the series using a narrator to enhance the dramatic narrative.

Further written or verbal announcement may include the synopsis of each mini-drama, listed on pages 9-10 to help the audience prepare for that which they will experience.

1
An Elder And Peter Before The Passover

The Setting

Late afternoon on a Jerusalem street near the marketplace. If properties are desired, a background canvas can portray several buildings.

Costumes

Peter — colorful, striped robe, to ankles. Brown sandals. Red, curly, long hair and red beard. If possible, Peter should be a tall, burly man.

Elder — simple, light brown or tan robe, to ankles, free flowing. Sandals. Dark hair, neatly trimmed, with dark beard. If possible, the Elder should be short and somewhat chubby.

Directions

The sound effects of noises in a marketplace open the scene, with no one on stage. After fifteen to twenty seconds of sound effects, Elder enters, stage right, and walks to center stage. Sound effects diminish to background noise and continue softly until Peter enters and the conversation begins.

Sound Effects

Marketplace noises. Loud.

Elder enters, walks slowly from stage right to center stage to speak directly to audience. Sound effects fade to background noise.

Elder: I ... I just don't know. Things are certainly in an uproar this week. The other day when we elders met with the chief priests, the consensus was that we arrest the carpenter from Nazareth named Jesus-bar-Joseph and kill him. *(Pause)* I hate the business of killing any man. *(Pause)* He is a nuisance, though, I guess. Yes, a nuisance, if nothing more. *(Pause. Looks thoughtfully, as if wondering whether he believes that or not.)* At any rate, we at least decided we'd not arrest the carpenter during the feast, lest we cause a riot among the people here in Jerusalem for the Passover. *(Shudders)* What a calamity that would be with all these pilgrims here!

Elder begins to pace back and forth, slowly, as he continues.

That carpenter — he's something else, all right!. It's certain that Caiaphas and most of the priests and other elders consider him a dangerous man. He ... he seems to be trying to reform our religion — or ruin it! — and the priests aren't very tolerant of that! *(Pause)* Besides, things are pretty good the way they are. I've got no complaints. None at all. I like my life the way it is, and I don't see why the carpenter appeals to so many people ... at least not from what I've heard about him. He seems to appeal to people who are dissatisfied with life. And I simply cannot see why anyone is dissatisfied. After all, if a man is poor and doesn't like being poor, let him pull himself out of poverty.

Elder stops pacing. Looks thoughtfully for a long time, shakes his head, and continues, looking directly at audience.

Yet, this carpenter fellow ... I ... I just can't get him out of my mind. I saw what he did the other day in the Temple. Ghastly! I wanted to punch him in the nose right there myself, but I really don't like fisticuffs. And that crowd ... *(With extreme disgust)* they really loved it, most of them. Petty commoners! I just don't see any of that kind of roughhousing, no matter what the cause.

Elder turns toward stage right, as if to begin pacing again, but remains stationary. Peter enters, stage left, walks slowly, looks about as if hunting for a certain house. As Peter nears Elder, Elder turns abruptly, as if in thought, and the two bump into each other.

Peter: Oh! Pardon me, sir. *(Excitedly)* But, I'm quite preoccupied in hunting a certain house …

Elder: *(Looking curiously at Peter)* That's all right, my good man. I … I was lost in thought myself and not paying much attention to where I was going.

Peter: *(Starting off)* I'll be on my way, then …

Elder: *(Following)* Wait a minute, my good man. You … uh … you wouldn't happen to be one of the companions of the carpenter from Nazareth … I believe his name is Jesus.

(Sound effects fade slowly out.)

Peter: *(Stops, turns abruptly to Elder and says with excitement)* Yes, indeed, I am! I am Simon, called the Rock by the Master himself.

Elder: The Master?

Peter: Yes, sir. We call Jesus, Master.

Elder: Indeed! *(Musing)* Master, eh?

Peter: Yes! *(With great excitement)* Have you not heard of his teachings, sir? Have you not heard him speak of love as the fulfillment of all the commandments? Have you not seen him heal, at an instant? On our way to Jerusalem, just the other day, he healed a blind man at Jericho just by saying, "Your faith has made you well." Have you ever seen him? Looked into his eyes? Those eyes … oh, sir, they are so deep, so understanding, so compassionate, so loving. He can look at you and you feel that he knows you inside out — and that he doesn't condemn you for whatever sins you have committed. He … *(With great excitement)* he makes you feel free! The Master he is, sure enough. The Master of all teachers … for he is the One we've waited for so long … *(Trails off …*

suddenly aware that he is talking to a stranger. Then, politely) By the way, good sir, who are you?

Elder: I am the elder, Eli-bar-Jonah. *(Sensing Peter's hesitancy)* But, you needn't worry, Simon. I am quite interested in this Master of yours and I count it good fortune, indeed, that we have ... uh ... *(Smiling in a friendly way)* literally bumped into each other this day. Indeed, all of Jerusalem is interested in your carpenter friend. That was, incidentally, some parade you fellows pulled off the other day when your Master rode into the city. Tell me more about this man who can inspire such ... such devotion in you.

Peter: *(Hesitancy gone. Excitedly)* I'd be happy to, sir. I'll begin ...

Elder: Begin, please, by telling me exactly what happened in the Temple on Monday.

Peter: *(Grimly, with determination)* It's about time somebody put a stop to that ... that robbery of the poor pilgrims who come here from all over the world for the Festival. The Master cannot stand to see the poor fleeced by the rich ... and supposedly in the Name of the Holy One, but really only for the pockets of those petty thieves who call themselves ...

Elder: *(Looking around anxiously)* Careful, man! They could have your head for that!

Peter: *(Angrily)* Nobody's going to have anybody's head, sir ... My Master is going to be King ... in a kingdom of love and peace. There'll be no such thing as executions and killing then.

Elder: *(With surprise)* Your Master is going to be king?

Peter: Indeed he is, sir. That's what he has promised, and he has always kept his promises. *(With excitement)* We are all so anxious for it to happen ...

Elder: Precisely when does your Master propose to take over the kingdom?

Peter: I … uh … I don't know for sure …

Elder: You seem to be hesitating. Are you not telling me what you know?

Peter: Well … sir … the truth is … I … I don't know for sure. *(Excitedly)* But, we do know that it is soon … the time is near … very, very near!

Elder: So you think he's going to be king, eh?

Peter: Right! He is going to be king in a kingdom of love and peace and prosperity. And I … *(Almost too excited to talk)* I am going to be right there with him … I and the others who have served him will be his right-hand men in ruling his kingdom. Oh, it will be so fantastic: peace and love and prosperity!

Elder: *(Cynically)* Do you know anything about government?

Peter: We don't need to know anything about government. Don't you see? My Master's teachings on love and peace won't require armies or weapons or government departments … *(Acts as if suddenly he is struck by reality)* … at least not after a time when everyone accepts his teachings.

Elder: *(Coyly, realizing Peter has trapped himself)* Meanwhile, how does your Master propose to take over the government and rule … until people accept his teachings?

Peter: *(Stunned)* That … that he … he has not yet revealed to us, sir.

Elder: *(Still coyly)* It seems a grandiose plan to me … and quite dangerous! What, by the way, does your Master propose to do about Pilate and Herod and the Roman Empire's control over us? Rome doesn't take kindly to the idea of rebellion.

Peter: *(Puzzled)* I ... uh ... I really don't know. *(Suddenly excited again)* But, I imagine that they, too, will accept my Master's teachings and there'll be ... there'll be no problem at all.

Elder: *(Surprised)* Do you really believe all that? Do you really believe that all Jews and all Romans will listen to your ... your carpenter from Nazareth and just quietly let him become a king?

Peter: *(Excitedly)* Of course! I ... I don't know quite how, but he has ... *(Catching himself)* ... he has great power. Sir, you must hear him teach. I have never heard anything so beautiful. I have never seen anything so wondrous as the things he does. I have never found anything as helpful as his teachings. There is just no other way to live! He has done so much for me ... just being close to him, just listening to him ... just watching him and feeling his presence. Why ... I'd ... I'd do anything ... anything at all for him and for his kingdom.

Elder: *(Cautiously, sensing a chance to test Peter's loyalty)* You'd do ... anything ... anything at all for the carpenter, eh?

Peter: Oh, yes sir! Anything at all! *(His excitement grows)* I'd ... I'd live in the desert ... I'd walk all the roads in Judea again and again ... I'd defend him ... I'd ... I'd even die for him.

Elder: Your loyalty is astonishing, Simon, and quite admirable. *(Slowly, cautiously)* Have you heard, Simon, some of the rumors in the city this week?

Peter: Rumors?

Elder: *(Still slowly, cautiously)* Yes, I've heard some ... uh ... ugly rumors that your ... uh ... Master's teachings are stirring up the people. *(Very slowly, eyeing Peter intently)* I've ... I've even heard rumbles that the people may rise up against him.

Peter: *(Angry)* Rise up against him? The people love him! Perhaps it's the priests …

Elder: *(Interrupting Peter)* Tell me, Simon, have you not heard the rumor that your Master's … uh … way-out ideas … kind of revolutionary ideas … simply don't fit in our society and the people don't like that?

Peter: *(Angry)* Ridiculous! The only ones who don't like my Master's ideas are the pr …

Elder: *(Interrupting again)* Calm down, my good man! You needn't get so worked up. I'm only talking about rumors … that's all … and you know what rumors can do to truth.

Peter: *(Forcibly, visibly calming himself down. Paces a bit)* You are right. There's no … no reason to get so upset. My apologies.

Elder: *(Kindly)* Indeed, I can understand, Simon. You who are so utterly devoted to the carpenter would get upset over any such rumors. *(Pause. Then slowly, carefully)* You said that your Master is to be … to be king. I noticed a hint in your voice that suggested you feel he may be … may be … the … uh … *(Very softly, confidentially)* the Messiah.

Peter: *(Stunned, cautious)* Oh? Did … did I say that? *(Peter stands tensely as Elder begins his reply)*

Elder: *(Aware that he has trapped Peter)* You … well, you hinted at it. And what I'm getting at is this. I want the Messiah to come, too. I'd give anything to have the Son of David here, right now, *(Almost a whisper)* to overthrow those filthy Romans and to conquer other nations, so that we could have peace and prosperity and rule ourselves … *(Elatedly)* and perhaps the whole world.

Peter begins to relax, smile and nod in agreement with Elder.

Elder: Just think how wealthy we would be. I'd have four times as many slaves as I have now. And we'd be so strong that no other nation would try to conquer us. How beautiful it all would be. *(Brief pause)* But, this ... this Master of yours ... he is not trained in city ways, nor educated in government, nor trained in warfare. He's uneducated, country-bred, unskilled in these important matters. How could he ever accomplish what the Messiah is to do? How *(Indignant with anger)* in the world can you consider him to be the long-awaited One?

Peter: *(Trapped, but unaware of it, exuberantly)* Oh, sir, but he is ... he is the Messiah. Jeremiah and Isaiah have pointed very clearly to what the Messiah will be and my Master fits the description. He brings good news to the poor; he gives sight to the blind, hearing to the deaf; he makes the lame man walk. And his teachings ... every word he utters is of the love of God for us ... all of us ... you and me ... no matter how rich or how poor we are! That ... that means that he must be the Messiah ... the one who comes to fulfill the law and the prophets.

Elder: But ... but I understand that your carpenter friend proposes that we throw out the law and the prophets. That's why we ... *(Catches himself abruptly)* ... that's why the people are so upset.

Peter: Not throwing them out, sir. My Master has come to fulfill them ... to complete them ... to bring in a whole new age of love and peace in people's hearts. The Master himself has given us a new commandment ... that we love one another as he has loved us. And, sir, he has spent his love so freely on all of us ... even on strangers. No matter how tired he is, he will listen to and speak to and help anyone who seeks him out. He even ... now get this ... he even urges little children to come near and talk to him.

Elder: Well, I've nothing against children, of course. But this ... this whole idea of his ... this whole idea that he is the Messiah come to free us from oppression and bring in peace and prosperity

… it's absurd. He's just a country bumpkin. It'll never work! He … he just cannot be the Messiah. All he'll do is cause trouble … *(Pauses thoughtfully)* … trouble, that's all.

Peter: But, sir, you are wrong. It will work. The Master urges it. And he is … yes, he is the Christ, the Son of the living God. And I … I'm right there … I'll do anything I can to see that what he teaches does work. *(Abrupt pause)* Oh, sir, excuse me, but I must be going. The Master has sent me to find a certain house where we will eat Passover together, and I don't want to let him down. Good-day, sir. *(Exits stage right, in a rush)*

(Sound effects of marketplace noise come in low as Peter exits and build slightly.)

Elder: *(Walks to stage center slowly. Pauses. Looks over audience, then speaks directly to audience.)* Well … we shall see … we shall see … *(Throws hands out and up in a gesture of wonder)* … we shall see …

Elder turns, walks slowly toward stage left and out.

(Sound effects continue to build for several seconds, then are cut off.)

2
Judas And Mary Magdalene After The Last Supper

The Setting

Night on a Jerusalem street. Properties may include background painting of a first century building, at which point Judas and Mary will then meet. Normally, no properties are required.

Costumes

Judas — colorful robe, preferably stripes in bright colors. Sandals. Long hair combed back and down neck, with short, neat beard.

Mary — flowing robe of black and white. Veil of same material, white, to cover hair. Sandals. A sparkling ring or two on her hands.

Directions

The narrator is unseen by the audience. He reads his lines from backstage, offstage, or from the rear of the auditorium.

When the drama begins, all lights should be off in the room, save for stage lights indicating night, on the stage or chancel. Lights which can be set to create eerie shadows will heighten the drama once lights are properly set. Permit ten to fifteen seconds of darkness and quiet before the narrator reads his opening lines.

Narrator: "... Jesus ... was deeply troubled, and declared openly: 'I tell you the truth: one of you is going to betray me.' The disciples looked at one another, completely puzzled about whom he meant. One of the disciples ... asked, 'Who is it, Lord?' Jesus answered, 'I will dip the bread in the sauce and give it to him; he is the man.' So he took a piece of bread, dipped it, and gave it to Judas, the son of Simon Iscariot. As soon as Judas took the bread, Satan went into him. Jesus said to him, 'Hurry and do what you must!' ... Judas accepted the bread and went out at once. It was night."

Judas enters from left. He half runs, half sneaks, stumbles occasionally. He goes back and forth across stage in this manner two or three times. As he does this, he looks about himself constantly, as if afraid of being pursued or captured. On about the third trip across the stage as he is moving stage right to left, Mary Magdalene appears, as if from nowhere. Judas jumps, startled.

Mary: Why, Judas! I did not expect to see you out here at this hour tonight.

Judas stares briefly at Mary, then looks around quickly, as if wishing he could have avoided her. Then he says:

Judas: Nor I you, Mary of Magdala.

Mary: *(Studies Judas a moment, as Judas continues looking nervously all about)* Are … are you all right, Judas? You've been running. *(Anxiously)* Is … is something wrong? It's not …

Judas: *(Suddenly drawing himself up, pulling himself together)* No, Mary, no … not a thing is wrong. Why must you women wonder if something's wrong all the time?

Mary: Now, Judas, we're just concerned. I am relieved to hear you say that nothing is wrong, though. For a moment, I thought perhaps … perhaps something was wrong with the Master.

Judas: *(Quickly, still looking around)* No … no … nothing is wrong with the Master, Mary. He's … quite all right.

Mary: *(Looking puzzled)* I'm so glad to hear that. But you, Judas, you don't seem to be yourself this evening.

Judas: *(Looking around)* Oh, me … I … I'm fine, Mary. Fine.

Mary: And what is the Master doing this evening? I haven't seen him since the other day after all that trouble over the Temple incident.

Judas: *(With disdain)* Yes, that was some incident. The Master certainly did perform well. I ... I must go, Mary ... I ...

Mary: But Judas, you haven't answered my question. What is the Master doing tonight?

Judas: *(Lost. Far away. Staring)* Tonight?

Mary: *(Impatiently)* Yes, Judas, tonight! Why ... Why, it is the Passover. *(Slightly alarmed)* Judas, why aren't you with the Master for Passover?

Judas: *(Shocked back to reality)* I ... I was, Mary. It's ... it's all over ... *(Slight pause, then quietly)* ... all over.

Mary: *(Alarmed)* What's all over, Judas?

Judas: Why ... uh ... what did you say?

Mary: *(Indignantly)* Judas, you said, "It's all over." What's all over? The Passover meal?

Judas: *(Again recovered to reality)* Yes, Mary ... that's it ... the Passover meal. *(Looking around again)* Well, Mary, nice to see you. I must get going ... I ... I'm ...

Mary takes hold of his arms, keeping him in place.

Mary: Wait a minute, Judas. I've been wanting to talk to one of you who are with the Master all the time, anyway. I ... I'm really worried about him ... about the rumors in this city. Have you heard them?

Judas: Rumors?

Mary: Yes ... I ... I can hardly believe them! I was just on my way to try to find the Master so I could warn him.

Judas: *(Anxiously and yet firmly)* Wait a minute, Mary. The Master is … uh … resting. He is … he's very tired. And besides, what do you want to go disturbing him about a lot of rumors for? I haven't heard any … uh … rumors. *(With anger)* Precisely what do these rumors say?

Mary: Calm down, Judas! I did not mean to make you angry. Your anger will do no good. I know that you love the Master as I do. *(Judas looks away from her)* And we don't want anything to happen to him. But anger will get us nowhere. Just calm down and we'll see how we can help him.

Judas looks nervously around, searching all about him as if expecting an intruder or trying to get away from Mary.

Judas: Help him? What help does he need? *(With sarcasm)* He can do anything.

Mary: *(Disregarding Judas' last remark)* The rumors are absolutely frightening … what they say will happen to the Master. I'm really scared. I get chills up and down my spine just thinking about it. They say that the Master is … *(Almost breaks into tears, voice shaky)* … is … going to be tried … and … executed … *(Angrily)* like a common criminal! How dare they? That's all this city's been talking about all week. I hear it in the marketplace and even in the Temple courtyard.

Judas: *(Working hard at being casual, but still looking about)* Oh, Mary! You women! Where do you dig up those horror stories? *(Intently)* What, in the name of the God of Abraham and Isaac, could anyone ever try to execute the Master for?

Mary: I don't understand it either, Judas. I cannot imagine! At first, I didn't believe the rumors. I … I sort of laughed at them. But then I became truly afraid. Now I am trying very hard to see what basis anyone might have for wanting to harm him. Just take me as one example of the good that he has done. Not too many months ago, I suffered from nerves that were grim beyond description. *(Exaltedly)* He healed me! He's wonderful! *(Calming down somewhat, but with exaltation)* And he's done so much for so many others. Just what he teaches is enough to make the world a different place to live in. He's made life different for me, Judas, and for many others. For you, too, Judas.

Judas stares at her briefly. Mary looks at him, as Narrator reads. Mary does not hear Narrator. Judas fidgets with his hands and feet as Narrator reads, but otherwise stares at Mary.

Narrator: "When the hour came, Jesus took his place at the table with the apostles. And he said to them: 'I have wanted so much to eat this Passover meal with you before I suffer! For I tell you, I will never eat it until it is given its real meaning in the Kingdom of God.' Then Jesus took the cup, gave thanks to God, and said, 'Take this and share it among yourselves; for I tell you that I will not drink this wine from now on until the Kingdom of God comes.' Then he took the bread, gave thanks to God, broke it, and gave it to them, saying, 'This is my body … which is given for you. Do this in memory of me.' In the same way he gave them the cup, after the supper, saying, 'This cup is God's new covenant sealed with my blood which is poured out for you….' "

When Narrator concludes, Judas shakes his head fiercely, as if trying to clear his mind.

Mary: *(Concerned)* Judas … are … are you all right?

Judas: *(Again back to reality)* Oh! Oh, yes. *(Smiles)* Yes, I am. And … and you're right, Mary, the Master has … has made a difference … quite a difference … in my life.

Mary: Then, don't you think that these others … these people who are apparently trying to harm the Master … should have an opportunity to understand him better? I know it takes time for some people to understand him. And I just know that if they'd take the time, all people could come to understand him, love him, and profit from his teachings. They'd never listen to a woman, either ... but wouldn't they listen to you and Peter and James and the rest, if you went to them?

Judas: *(Far away again)* Listen to us?

Mary: *(Unaware that Judas has drifted off. He continues to look around nervously while she speaks)* Yes, Judas, listen to you ... if you spoke of the wonders of the Master, if you told them all the things he's done for people. I'm sure they don't know the whole story. They just think he doesn't like some things in the Temple. And they think he's against taxes — which he isn't. If they just knew the whole truth ...

Judas: *(Inserts)* Truth ... truth ... truth? *(As Mary goes on, not hearing Judas)*

Mary: ... they'd feel a lot differently about him. And there are so many people, besides you twelve, to testify of what he has done for them. But, well, whatever we can do tomorrow or the next day ... or even now, if there is any basis at all to those rumors. We'd better warn the Master immediately until we have time to take some action.

Mary takes one step, toward stage right, reaching for Judas' hand to take him along. As she starts, Judas pulls her back, uses both hands gently but firmly to hold her in place, then releases her.

Judas: For heaven's sake, Mary. You women get too upset over rumors ... simple, stupid, idle gossip that you pick up here and there and distort in your minds. Such imaginations you have! It all means nothing, whatever the rumors you heard. There's nothing to warn the Master about. No sense upsetting him over nothing but idle gossip. Be ... be ... besides ... he's tired ... and he's ... uh ... resting now.

Mary: *(Indignantly)* But, Judas, those rumors are not unfounded. That's what scares me. The people in this city, at least some of them, are quite vindictive; quite intent. Some are downright angry and threatened by the Master. I've heard some influential people say that he is an agent of Satan, that his wonderful words are black magic, and that they'll have none of that here. Another one I heard in the marketplace saying that the Master is trying to ruin religion by throwing out the law and the prophets. And was he ever mad! And then, I heard a little group of people buzzing like bees, all excited, stomping their feet, waving their arms, and cursing … and they kept muttering … "He's a madman. He's a blasphemer. Death to blasphemers!"

Judas: *(Far away. Slowly)* Death … to … blasphemers …

Mary: *(Still unaware that Judas has drifted from the conversation)* That's right, Judas. That's exactly what they've been saying. And I think we have to act now.

Judas: *(Still far away as he speaks. Looks around. When he looks at Mary, he does not really see her. Keeps his head in almost continual motion as he speaks.)* Not everything can be done now, Mary, it's … it's … a holiday. Surely you understand, too, that … that these things the Master says and does are new. People just don't go for new things right away.

Mary: But, they've just got to be patient. He is no blasphemer. *(Angrily)* And he's not a madman, either. Some good things take time … a lot of time.

Judas: Yes … a lot of time … a lot of time. *(Stops looking around and looks at Mary briefly. Then, staring blankly in her direction)* But, people just aren't patient. I've … I've … been with the Master three years now … and he has accomplished … *(Pause)* … accomplished … so … so little …

Mary: *(Stunned and angry)* So little? Judas, you've seen the healings. You've seen the changed lives. You know my story. And there are so many others. How ... *(Stops short, suddenly alarmed and suspicious)* How ... can you say he has accomplished so little?

Judas stares at floor. Mary looks at him intently.

Judas: *(Still staring at floor)* So ... little ... it seems that his kingdom is never going to come about ... he just doesn't take the initiative ... and I'm the treasurer ... Ha! ... There's never any money ... for us ... He insists that we give it away ... to the poor, he says. Poor. That's us. We're the ones that have to beg ... we're the ones that are poor. No money ... no power ... no peace ...

Mary: *(Uncertainly, but in an attempt to jar Judas to reality)* Money is no problem, Judas. I have substantial means, as you know, and I will gladly contribute even more generously to the Master.

Judas: *(Still staring at floor)* More ... yes, more ... more money ... more power ... more peace ... all seems futile ... all is vain. *(Brief pause)*

Mary becomes extremely nervous and uneasy. She looks intently at Judas, who slowly looks up from the floor and stares at her.

Judas: *(Staring blankly at, but not seeing Mary)* All is vain. Empty promises. He promises this ... that ... great promises ... and nothing ever comes of them ... *(Screams)* Nothing! *(Quickly calms down)* Nothing is changed ... where is our government of peace? Our prosperity? All ... is ... vain ...

Mary: *(Thoroughly shaken)* All is not vain, Judas. But ... quickly, time is passing, and we must act. *(Reaches for his hand)* Come, Judas, let us warn the Master.

Judas stares at her. She shakes him slightly by the hand. At first he continues to stare, then looks as if he is back to the reality of her presence. He shakes loose of her, looks around nervously.

Judas: *(Far away, but intently, quickly)* Well ... uh ... the Master sent me on an ... an errand ... I mean ... in a way he did ... and I'm on this ... this important errand ... and I've gotta go.

Mary: *(Shocked and angry)* Well, I'm going to warn the Master about these rumors. Nothing is more important than that. I'll go alone if you won't come. *(Judas begins to walk off toward stage left, is almost offstage as Mary finishes the following)* But, tell me, Judas, just where is he tonight?

Mary suddenly realizes that Judas is moving away. She looks startled, as if she might pursue, but then looks toward stage right instead, as if wondering where to go.

Judas: *(As he leaves the stage; loudly)* Important errand ... all is vain ... all ...

Mary: *(Suddenly turning her head to stage left — screams)* Judas!!! *(Slight pause, then dashes off, stage right).*

Alternate Ending

As Judas leaves stage, Narrator (unseen) reads while Mary remains in position.

Narrator: "Look, the Son of Man is now handed over to the power of sinful men."

Mary: *(Screams, looking to stage left)* Judas!!

Narrator: "Is it with a kiss, Judas, that you betray the Son of Man?"

Mary dashes off, stage right.

3
Caiaphas And Pilate's Wife Between The Trials

The Setting

A large, overstuffed chair, draped in gold or violet, at stage left. A smaller chair, with arms, set at an angle to effect easy, close conversation.

Costumes

Caiaphas — rich robe of bright colors. Sandals. Colorful turban wrapped around his head. One sparkling ring on each finger. Neatly trimmed beard.

Claudia — long white robe, with gold or silver cord tie as belt. Gold sandals. Hair piled high on her head, with tiara or other jeweled ornament. Sparkling necklace and several large, sparkling rings on both hands.

Directions

As the scene opens, stage is empty. Each character will make a self-introduction. Caiaphas enters, from stage left, stands stage center to speak to audience.

Caiaphas: I am Caiaphas, high priest in Jerusalem when your Jesus was crucified. To understand me at all, you have to understand that there was no such thing as separation of church and state in our Hebrew way of thinking. Ours was theocracy — God himself was our political as well as our spiritual head. He spoke through the kings, at one time; and now, in the time when Jesus lived, he spoke to us through his priests and prophets ... when we let his prophets speak!

But, there was, at that time, a peculiar twist in our system, brought about by Rome's oppression. We were a captive nation, politically, when Jesus of Nazareth met his doom. Yet, Rome let us go about our own business, religiously, so long as we did not try to revolt. This partial religious freedom was of the genius of the Roman Empire's success in keeping nations captive … and relatively calm.

Yet, we hated this system ferociously. We despised Rome and her interference in our affairs. That is, most of our people hated it, and inside they were seething, on the brink of revolt. So, it was my job, as chief priest, along with the other priests and our very handy army, to see that there was no rebellion or uprising. We priests had, rather cleverly I'd say, developed a knack for getting along with our Roman oppressors. And why not? Our jobs and wealth and influence depended upon our keeping Rome happy and the rabble-rousers in Jerusalem quiet and tame.

And that was quite a job! It wasn't the bed of roses some of your latter-day teachers would like to tell you it was. Your Jesus happened along and kind of filled the bill at the right moment for me. He was tending to rouse the people to rebellion, anyway. So, in turn, by rousing them against him, I let them get some of their venom and hatred toward Rome off their chest. They loved forcing Pilate's hand; and, most significant, for me, I got rid of … or, perhaps I should say, I *thought* I got rid of the biggest detriment to my religion's system and my own pocketbook who ever came along … Jesus, son of Joseph, the rabbi from Nazareth, who thought he was God.

Caiaphas pauses briefly, turns and slowly walks to overstuffed chair. Sits.

Claudia enters from stage right, slowly, regally. Stands stage center, speaks directly to audience.

Claudia: I am the wife of Pontius Pilate. Your Christian tradition later gave me the name of Claudia Procula. When my husband was assigned to be governor of Judea, I was heartsick. The Jews were the roughest of all Rome's conquered peoples to handle. And Judea! It was the end of the world, beyond civilization, so far as I was concerned; a boring place of desolation after the pomp and grandeur and thrill of Rome. But, we went; there was no choice. At least I did get to live in the Herodian palace, which was a far sight better and grander than anything else in town.

One thing I can say for Jerusalem, though: it was at least a lively and swinging place once a year at the Jews' festival of Passover. It was colorful and exciting to watch the spectacle from my windows high above the city. The religion of the Jews intrigued me — unofficially, of course. My husband and I were forced to worship Caesar publicly. Pontius was always quite nervous and tense when there were so many natives in town, and in high enough spirits at Passover to be sparked to rebel by a good rabble-rouser. That would have sent Pontius' career up in smoke. Above all things, he had to keep the Jews subdued and not let them rebel.

The year that we are concerned with … the year that your Jesus was executed … was a particularly restless year, for the rumors of this man who claimed to be a king of the Jews had built up to a point that Pontius was more nervous and more tense than usual. As you would say, he had an itchy trigger finger; he was overly sensitive to every noise and rumble and rumor. He had his aides continually on the prowl throughout the city to hear everything that was going on. He was not at all relieved, of course, when Jesus of Nazareth came to town for this Passover festival. He worried day and night about possible rebelling, and scarcely slept that week at all.

But, to me, your Jesus was intriguing. He was so much the opposite of all that I had known in Rome. What he taught was so alien to all that I had seen and lived. So, I was, therefore, curious about him.

Claudia pauses briefly, then turns and slowly walks to chair. Sits. After a brief pause, Caiaphas speaks.

Caiaphas: Well, my lady, to what do I owe the honored privilege of your presence … especially at this quite early hour?

Claudia: This carpenter … this rabbi … *(Nervously)* … what's his name … Jesus of Nazareth …

Caiaphas: You, my lady, are up and out about the city at this hour because of a nobody Jewish carpenter who thinks he's a rabbi … this Jesus?

Claudia: Yes, Caiaphas … because of Jesus of Nazareth. I understand that you have just … just encountered him …

Caiaphas: Indeed, I have, my lady. He was … *(Pauses. Looks intently at Claudia, warily, unsure of her)* … he was here, yes.

Claudia: What have you done with him?

Caiaphas: Done with him?

Claudia: *(Indignant with anger)* Cut out the games, priest! Servants talk … even your servants … and they talk to my servants … and the palace … indeed, the city is buzzing with rumors that this … this Jesus of Nazareth has been given the death sentence.

Caiaphas: My lady, you are aware, I presume, that it is unlawful for us Jews to put anyone to death.

Claudia: *(Still angry)* Your coyness and cleverness do not fool me, priest! Certainly you know that we are aware of your game of playing both ends against the middle — playing whatever role you think you need to play to get along with your own people and also with Rome. And, *(Smiles viciously)* certainly it doesn't hurt your pocketbook, either.

Caiaphas: *(Affronted, but controlled)* No offense, my lady …

Claudia: Put the politeness aside. I am deadly earnest in finding out about this Jesus. You have not answered my questions. *(Pause. No one speaks. Caiaphas looks her in the eye.)* Answer it honestly, please. I'll not be causing you any trouble with Pontius; you have my word on that.

Caiaphas: This Jesus ... this so-called prophet ... the man from the sticks, a nobody whom you've suddenly taken an interest in, my lady ... was duly tried by our tribunal, the Sanhedrin. He is a blasphemer against our God. As is proper, we have sent him to your husband for confirmation of our judgment.

Claudia: Have you sent him yet?

Caiaphas: He's on his way now ... just left a short time ago.

Claudia: Why, Caiaphas? Why did you sentence him to death?

Caiaphas: How much do you know about Jesus?

Claudia: *(Taken aback. She does not want her knowledge to show)* Know about him? Why ... why ... why hardly anything. I just heard all the commotion and the rumors this week, and I'm curious ... just curious.

Caiaphas: *(Slow smile spreads across his face as he speaks)* So ... that's it, eh ... Well, haven't you heard that he is teaching that there is a Heaven ... a life after this life, where the spirit of man will go forever ... providing, of course, that the man believes in this Jesus.

Claudia: And for that you ask death?

Caiaphas: *(Annoyed, but controlled)* Have you not heard what he did at the money tables in the Temple this week? He ruined the place, and now some of the pilgrims are refusing to exchange their currency.

Claudia: And for that you ask death?

Caiaphas: *(More annoyed, obviously showing how difficult it is to maintain control)* And, there's more. People ... all sorts of people claim that he has healed them of deafness, of muteness, of palsy, of nervous disorders … even of leprosy. At least, those are the rumors we hear.

Claudia: Well … has he?

Caiaphas: *(Gives a start, obviously controls himself)* Of course not, my lady. That is all … all ridiculous. Only God can heal. And most of the people who have made such claims were just imagining their maladies anyway.

Claudia: Like leprosy? How can one imagine leprosy?

Caiaphas: That was probably a put-up job. If nothing else, it's all black magic … the power of evil in this troublesome carpenter, fighting against our God.

Claudia: Even so, he's harmless, so far as I can tell.

Caiaphas: Well, my lady, it is your privilege to think that. But, we have been struggling many years for our faith and he upsets the whole nation.

Claudia: How is that?

Caiaphas: I am of the Sadducee party. We believe that the Pentateuch …

Claudia: *(Interrupts)* Pentateuch?

Caiaphas: That is the Book of Moses, the first five books of scripture: Genesis, Exodus, Leviticus, Numbers and Deuteronomy. These are the highest and holiest guides for our living. We believe that here is where our God tells us how to live now. And there is only now. There is no afterlife, no resurrection, as this Jesus claims; there are no angels, no spirits, none of this stuff he talks about. He simply cannot be let loose to destroy our teachings and faith with his blasphemy.

Claudia: Be that as it may, you've no reason to ask death for him. There are hundreds of others teaching different things and arguing this point or that.

Caiaphas: *(Frustrated, but again, controlled)* But, my lady, at the trial … that was the final straw. At the trial, *(Becomes angrier as he continues)* I myself asked Jesus, "Are you the Christ, the Son of the Blessed?" And he said, "I am." *(Dramatic, angry pause)* "I am." That is blasphemy against the Highest! Only death is suitable for one who claims to be Divine.

Claudia: There are a lot of people with a few bolts loose, running around claiming all sorts of things. You don't ask execution for them. Besides, what will you do with all the people who believe him?

Caiaphas: No one in the Sanhedrin believes him anything but a death-deserving madman. Public opinion is definitely against him.

Claudia: But, what about his circle of close associates? I hear there are about a dozen men who are so utterly devoted that they are willing to die for him.

Caiaphas: *(Facetiously, with mockery and triumphant smile)* Close circle of associates, my lady, willing to die for him? Ha-ha. One of those so-called associates turned him over to us … he even led my soldiers right to Jesus, and then kissed the motley carpenter on the cheek, so we'd be sure to get the right man … all for a small price, of course. And we've not been able to find one … not one man who will admit to even knowing this Jesus, let alone admit to being close to him. "Never saw him before" is the phrase we've heard all night long.

(Single crowing of a cock.)

Claudia: What do you think of Jesus, priest?

Caiaphas: I have just told you, my lady. He is a blasphemer ... a no-good troublemaker ... who just might *(Vicious smile)* just might even have led our people to rebellion. And that, I daresay, would have caused your husband no end of grief. *(Pause. Looks at her curiously, smiles knowingly and asks)* Why, my lady, are you so curious?

Claudia: I ... well, I might as well tell you, priest. I've had a dream ... a horrible, horrible dream ... a nightmare beyond anything I've ever dreamed.

Caiaphas: A dream?

Claudia: *(Upset)* A terrifying dream. Out of a black, thunderous, billowing sky, a horrible red ... the red of blood ... pours faster and faster ... gushing, rushing, and reddening the whole world. And then ... *(She shudders)* ... then there comes the most agonizing and pitiful cry that I have ever heard ... the cry of someone hurt ... someone innocent ... I awakened in a sweat, and with a scream, myself.

Caiaphas: It must have been a horrible dream, my lady. But, it has nothing to do with Jesus of Nazareth.

Claudia: Oh, but it does. When I awoke with this scream, I immediately said, "Jesus" — a name I scarcely knew until this week ... and then I realized that my dream tied in with the rumors I had heard about Jesus. When my servants told me the news of Jesus' trial here, I was certain beyond doubt that my dream meant that no one should harm this man ... for the sake of all of us.

Caiaphas: Come now, my lady. You're stretching the point. One carpenter from Nazareth is of no consequence. Besides, he is guilty of blasphemy.

Claudia: No, priest. You are wrong. You have to be wrong. Often before I have had such dreams ... and they have proved right. This

Jesus is innocent. You must not sentence him to death. He must live. I'm not sure why. But, I just know it to be so.

Caiaphas: *(As if to dismiss the whole matter)* The sentence is passed; it is done. Whatever happens now is up to your husband, the governor. *(Pause. Curious, sly smile)* By the way, you do seem terribly interested in this carpenter.

Claudia: *(Affronted)* I am interested only in justice, priest!

Caiaphas: And perhaps in your husband's career as well, should the people revolt because of Jesus' death.

Claudia: Watch yourself, priest. Remember who I am.

Caiaphas: *(With slight mockery)* A thousand apologies, my lady.

Claudia: *(Ignoring his mockery)* And what about ... what about the trial before Pontius?

Caiaphas: I am sure that the governor will agree with us.

Claudia: Then I shall go at once to him. When I tell him of my dream, he'll free the carpenter. He'll have nothing to do with the blood of an innocent man ... Good-day, priest. *(Exits stage right)*

Caiaphas: Good-day, my lady! *(Stands, pauses briefly. Walks slowly to stage center, addresses audience directly)* I, too, shall be going ... also to Pilate's courtyard ... to make sure that there is a crowd there to demand Jesus' death. Pilate's hands are tied. He'll have no choice but to go along with the mob, for he always releases one prisoner on the festival. We'll just make sure that a different one goes free. Pilate will have to execute this ... this troublesome carpenter. We've got to get rid of Jesus. He's a menace ... a menace to the faith.

Caiaphas exits rapidly stage left. As he leaves stage, just offstage, he shouts loudly:

Caiaphas: "It is expedient that one man die for the people."

4
Simon of Cyrene And Herod After The Trials

The Setting

Just inside the gate to the courtyard of Herod's Jerusalem residence. If properties are desired, a stone bench and some plants may be placed at stage center.

Costumes

Simon — simple robe, brown or beige. Sandals. Long hair, beard. White or brown cord may be used as belt, if desired.

Herod — bright, colorful robe, to ankles. Gold sandals. Several sparkling rings on his fingers. Short hair, no beard. He may be made up to look about 45 or 50.

Directions

When the lights are made ready for the scene, Simon appears from stage right and walks to the entrance of the courtyard. He stands there, looking to stage rear during sound effects.

Sound Effects

The noise of a rather large crowd, cheering, making noise of any sort. Some booing would be appropriate. Loud for ten to fifteen seconds, then fading away as narrator (unseen) begins. Slowly fade out during narration. Simon remains in position until narrator indicates Herod's entrance.

Narrator: Simon, the man from Cyrene, whose name was to be heard in Christian churches the world over from Good Friday until the end of time, was in Jerusalem for the Passover. Sensing the commotion about Herod's residence, he stopped to see what was going on. He was entranced by the scene and remained even after the crowd had dispersed. He didn't know exactly what was happening — and perhaps that is part of the reason he remained at the courtyard. He wanted to find out what *was* going on.

Herod enters, stage left.

Narrator: Suddenly, Simon was facing Herod, just outside the residence. Herod, attempting to cool off after his bout with the condemned carpenter, was out for a stroll.

Herod walks toward Simon. Both are startled.

Herod: Who are you, fellow? And what are you loitering here for?

Simon: Beg pardon, Excellency. I am Simon, from Cyrene. I was just coming into the city for the Festival … and I noticed the commotion here. So I stopped to watch.

Herod: *(Irritated)* The commotion, as you call it, is over. Others have gone. Be on your way.

Simon: *(Politely, unwilling to move on)* Sir, ah, would it be out of order if I were to inquire who that man was whom you were … uh … interrogating?

Herod: You mean you haven't heard, fellow?

Simon: No, sir. I was just coming into town …

Herod: That was one Jesus of Nazareth, a carpenter's son, who claims to be a rabbi and claims, by the way, to be also a "King" of the Jews. It is obvious that he is nothing but a nuisance who is trying to stir up these people to rebel against Rome. And we've squelched him, you'll notice.

Simon: I've heard a little about him. But, what did he do? What will happen to him now?

Herod: He'll be sentenced …

Simon: Sentenced? For what, Excellency?

Herod: For attempting to incite people to rebellion against Rome … that's "for what"!

Simon: Sir, forgive my ignorance, but I know little of this man Jesus. I watched him a bit here. He … he seems so strong, in one way, and yet so gentle and so weak. I cannot see how he would incite people to rebellion.

Herod: Come now, fellow. *(Wry smile)* You Jews shouldn't take us for fools. Rome has not become master of the world by falling for gentle actions which are intended to cover up preparation for revolt. Besides that, your own people turned the Nazarene over to Pontius Pilate … and they asked the death penalty for him … I think the charge was blasphemy.

Simon: Blasphemy?

Herod: I do not pretend to understand all the nonsense about your native religion; but, as nearly as I could tell, it had something to do with claiming to be the Son of God … your God, I mean … something about your Messiah … and being this king of the Jews. That's what we had to squelch … the king business. Blasphemy is your problem. But, Caesar is king of the Jews, and no motley carpenter is about to usurp his place. We put a sure and good stop to that today. We cannot let a maniac like that Nazarene rile up people. It's … discomfiting, to say the least. Why, even your priests were upset with the way he's been stirring up trouble in the church.

Simon: What kind of trouble are the priests upset about?

Herod: Some claims people have made that he works miracles … miracles, mind you, feats of wonder beyond our human understanding.

Simon: I have heard, Excellency, that he heals and cures those who are unhealthy.

Herod: Poppycock! Idle gossip and troublesome rumors, that's all that is. Didn't you see him here just now? I tried to get him to perform a stunt — pardon me, miracle — for me ... and he couldn't.

Simon: Couldn't, sir?

Herod: *(Mocking)* Ha! I said to him, "There is an old lady over there, shrivelled up to nothing. Make her tall and strong and smooth-skinned and appealing to me." He just stared at me. *(With rising anger)* So I said, "Have pity on her, O King. Look how she suffers. Show us your power."

Simon: *(With anticipation)* And did he?

Herod: *(With contempt)* Did he, nothing! It's not a question of whether he did or did not. He cannot. He simply cannot. He's merely posing as a religious teacher in order to subvert the people ... to get them up in arms against Rome. That's what he's ... or, rather, that's what he *was* trying to do. And those bloody fools spread tales that he can do anything.

Simon: I have heard, Excellency, that he has calmed storms, and wilted a fig tree with a look.

Herod: Come, fellow, you've more sense than to believe that, surely!

Simon: But, Excellency, I have also heard it said that Jesus performs his works of wonder only upon those who have faith that he can help them.

Herod: That little shrivelled up old lady looked pleadingly at him. And he did nothing. So, I tried him again. I said, "If you are so powerful and, as you claim, divine, why didn't you stop your associate from turning you over to your high priest?"

Simon: Did he answer you?

Herod: He stared at me again. *(With rising anger)* All he did was stare, straight at me, straight through me, until my temper flared and I slapped his greasy face. *(Repeats striking of Jesus in air.)*

Simon: Did he not answer you at all?

Herod: Not at all. Not even to try to save his life. He's got to be mad. So, I finally determined to propose a solution to our dilemma of wondering what to do with him. I said, "If you are divine, bring that disciple … what's his name … well, whoever he is, here, this instant. Have him confess that he lied, that he made a mistake in turning you in … and I will release you."

Simon: *(With anticipation)* And what happened then?

Herod: He stared again! *(Hits hand with fist)*

Simon: You mean, Excellency, that he refused every avenue you offered him to show himself as what he … what others claim he is?

Herod: Precisely. He refused every offer to show the power he claims to have.

Simon: Did you ask about his teachings, Excellency? Although I've heard a bit about him, I had never seen him or heard him until today. I understand that he teaches love … love for God and love for our neighbors. It is said that he insists that all men are our neighbors, and as our neighbors, they deserve all that we can give them or do for them. I have heard that his teachings have helped many people find meaning in their lives.

Herod: Meaning? What is meaning? Life is life, short, brisk and futile. I don't know where you hear what you hear, fellow, but all I've heard is that he is trying to stir up a revolt. He does it, I'm told, by telling the poor that they are worth something. Ha! Of course they're not worth a thing. They're scum. All he wants to do is butter them up so they'll not only revolt, but make him their king.

Simon: But, I have heard that all he really desires is peace in men's hearts.

Herod: Since he wouldn't answer anything I asked him, I can hardly be certain that he intends anything — except, of course, rebellion. He's up to no good ... rather, he was up to no good. *(With rising anger)* And to have the audacity to refuse to answer my questions! What could I do with such contempt? *(Anger gives way to smirk)* So, I decided to play the game his way. I gave him the most beautiful kingly robe in my wardrobe ... bowed to him in obeisance ... and called him "King" — but, then, you probably heard that part.

Simon: Yes ... I saw them all bowing and curtseying, calling him "King" ...

Herod: And you noticed, I trust, that your priests and their henchmen were screaming their fool heads off, accusing him of everything in the book. What a sight it was! *(Gleeful smile)*

Simon: *(Sullenly)* Yes ... what a sight.

Herod: *(Ignoring Simon's previous remark)* And then we all had a good belly laugh over the whole thing. It turned out to be quite amusing, really. The day is made. I have sent him back to my friend Pilate.

Simon: How is it that Jesus came to you in the first place?

Herod: That, fellow, was the doing of Pilate. Pilate's worried that the stink that your court's death sentence upon this man will cause trouble ... and he's not about to take the rap for that kind of trouble.

But, that's hardly likely, with your priests even against him. So, Pilate found out that the carpenter is a Galilean and — pronto — sent him and the whole motley mob over here on the double, hoping I'd make some decision.

Simon: And you are sending him back, with no decision?

Herod: Right you are. The decision is in Pilate's hands. I've had my curiosity satisfied. Indeed, I'm glad Pilate sent him here. I've been ... well, curious ... just curious about the carpenter ever since the rumors began about him. I had the opportunity to see if he could do any of these things he's supposedly able to do. What an impostor!

Simon: What will happen to him now, Excellency?

Herod: Oh ... he'll get the cross, I suppose. For Pilate's not about to let him get away. Pilate will find some way to make sure that the Galilean is executed.

Simon: *(Horrified)* The cross? That's a horror I dare not imagine. *(Pause)* Why ... why, that carpenter will have a devil of a time carrying one of those crosses. They look so heavy and he ... he doesn't look that strong. He looked so pale and tired.

Herod: And that he should. He's been up the night through, what with his trial before your priests and then his meeting with Pilate and coming here.

Simon: *(Still horrified and somewhat stunned)* What a terrible punishment. *(Aside)* The cross ... too horrible, too heavy to bear ...

Herod: What was that you said, fellow?

Simon: *(Quickly)* Nothing ... nothing, Excellency. *(More slowly)* I am just ... just appalled at the thought of that tired man having to carry a heavy cross and then ... then have to suffer and die on it.

Herod: *(Flippantly)* Yes, 'tis a pity we have to deal so harshly with troublemakers. But, that's the way of this world. *(More seriously)* Be grateful that you are not in his place, fellow. He will have a long, hard, hot day ahead before he breathes his last. Those crosses are murder to carry …

Lights fade. Choir or solo voice sings the verse from "Go To Dark Gethsemane" which reads:

Follow to the judgment hall,
View the Lord of life arraigned;
O the wormwood and the gall!
O the pangs his soul sustained!
Shun not suffering, shame, or loss;
Learn of him to bear the cross.

5
Joseph Of Arimathea And Barabbas During The Crucifixion

The Setting

Countryside, just outside the walls of Jerusalem, near Calvary, during the late morning. Three silhouettes of crosses in the distance, toward stage right, would add an effective dimension to this setting.

Costumes

Barabbas — white toga (easily made in one piece from a white sheet), knee-length, tattered at sleeves, neck and along bottom, from wear and tear of prison, slightly dirty and smudged. Barabbas should be ruddy and somewhat dirty all over. Unshaven. Long, messy hair. Barefoot.

Joseph — long robe of bright colors, perhaps stripes. Sandals. Long hair, beard, both neatly trimmed. One large ring on left hand; two sparkling rings on right hand.

Directions

As scene opens, Joseph and Barabbas are both in position, stage center, looking toward stage right where the sound effects are intended to come from and where, if used, cross silhouettes are placed. Sound effects of crowd noises are at maximum. Narrator is unseen. It is most effective if his voice can come from direction of Calvary, stage right.

Sound Effects

Rowdy crowd, booing, cheering, making all sorts of noises, at very loud volume.

Joseph and Barabbas stand, backs to audience, looking toward stage right. Each occasionally shakes his head or wrings his hands.

Sound effects gradually diminish over period of about one minute, indicating that the crowd is moving away from the characters.

When sound effects have toned down to background noise level, Joseph and Barabbas slowly turn to face each other, as Joseph says:

Joseph: I … I just can't believe it. It's brutal. *(Pause)* Well, they must have reached the little hill by now; the noise is a lot less ear-breaking. *(Pause)* I just cannot believe that this is happening.

Barabbas: *(Somewhat cocky)* Nor I. I expected to be going to that little hill for my last trip today … and here I am instead. *(Pauses. Suddenly shakes his head in disbelief and subsequently smiles)* I … I really can't believe it, but hip-hip-hooray!

Joseph: *(Soberly)* Your good fortune, Barabbas, is the Nazarene's misfortune.

Barabbas: *(Somewhat cocky again)* I'll say. Lucky I was, that's sure, to have someone like that fool carpenter around to intrigue these people into wanting his blood instead of mine.

Joseph: *(Offended)* You're fortunate, yes … and not very deserving either. I'm told that you are a robber and a murderer and, even if I'm risking myself by saying so, you well do not deserve to be let off while Jesus is put to death.

Barabbas: What difference to you, man, whether it's me or him?

Joseph: A great deal of difference. I believe in justice. There goes up on that cross a man who is innocent — and you are guilty. There goes up on that cross a man for whom I have great respect, an admirable teacher, a man who is … *(Hesitates, uncertain as to word choice)* … who is … is … exceptional.

Barabbas: Exceptional? A carpenter? Ha! A man's a man, that's what, and there's none better than others, nor none worse, no matter what you say ... *(Looks quizzically at Joseph)* whoever you are.

Joseph: I am Joseph, of Arimathea.

Barabbas: *(Shrugging his shoulders)* So?

Joseph: *(Disgusted)* I simply told you because you asked. *(Pause)* And I'm not going to agree with your statement that a man's a man and all are alike. There are exceptional men, and Jesus of Nazareth is one of those exceptions.

Barabbas: *(Sarcastically)* Do tell me!

Joseph: *(Undaunted by Barabbas' attitude)* He is one of history's most unusual men, I'd say. I myself have listened to him and watched him. He is ... *(Hesitatingly)* ... he is ... I believe that he is ... the Messiah ... the long-awaited Messiah.

Barabbas: *(Shocked)* Him? That carpenter with the bleeding back and the crown of thorns and not a friend around to help him carry his cross even?

Joseph: Don't let outward appearances fool you, Barabbas.

Barabbas: *(Mocking)* Oh, yes, he ... is ... the ... Messiah. Come on, man. You gotta be kidding!

Joseph: *(Quite soberly)* No, I am not kidding. *(Pauses. Shakes his head)* I am convinced that he is ... that he is the Messiah ... And I ... I can never forgive myself that he's being crucified.

(Background noise of crowd stops.)

Joseph: *(Hand to ear)* What's that? The noise has stopped.

Narrator: "Father, forgive, for they don't know what they're doing."

(Background noise of crowd resumes.)

Barabbas: Well, the noise is back. But, I'm curious … curious, that's all. You were saying that you wouldn't forgive yourself that the carpenter's being crucified?

Joseph: That's right. I … oh, I shouldn't be telling you … but somehow I've got to tell somebody now … and you're the only one around. I … I'm a member of the Sanhedrin … and we all voted to condemn him to death.

Barabbas: So, you voted the way you thought it ought to be … all in the line of duty and all that.

Joseph: *(Looking at floor)* No, Barabbas, not the way I thought it ought to be. But the way I knew I had to vote if I was not to get in trouble with my … my colleagues. You see, I really do believe that Jesus of Nazareth is the Christ, the son of the Living God — the Messiah. *(Breaks into a sob)* But … I … I wasn't man enough to stand up and say so. *(Shakes his head a number of times as he says)* I … just … didn't have the … the guts.

Barabbas: Hey, man, don't let it grab you like that! It's over. Nothing you could do about it, anyway, if they was all against him. If I was with those guys, I'd do like they do, too. I mean, after all, we gotta look after our own skin, you know.

Joseph: That's not … that's not what Jesus teaches. He teaches that we give ourselves for others … that we lose our life so that others may find and have life.

Barabbas: You gotta be kidding again! There's no sense in that. An eye for an eye, and tooth for tooth, they say. Why … why, a man would be just plain dumb to do a thing like that. Not me, boy …

Joseph: *(Looks piercingly at Barabbas)* But Jesus did just that for you, Barabbas. He is innocent. You're the one with the eye for eye business coming to you.

Barabbas: *(Stunned momentarily, but quickly recovering)* Oh, sure, man, sure! Like he just walked right up there to old Pilate and voluntarily said, "Pilate, old boy, I'm here to take Barabbas' place. Let him go, Excellency, and take me up to that little old hill and put me on the cross you have set aside for him." Oh, brother! That's not the way I heard it. It was like that carpenter just didn't have no choice. That's the way I got it.

Joseph: Don't count on that "no choice" business. Besides, you are certainly sarcastic and flippant for a man whose life has just been given to him because another man is dying in his place.

Barabbas: *(Somewhat nervous)* Sarcastic ... no ... no ... just realistic. That's all, Joseph, old boy, just realistic. That's the way the chariot races, a lot of taking care of yourself and a little bit of luck. *(Braggingly)* And luck was sure with me today. Wow! I ... I ...

Joseph: Luck?

Barabbas: Yeah, luck. As I was about to say, last night was one hell of a night. I couldn't sleep; I couldn't eat — whenever I tried, I puked all over the cell. At every footstep, my heart beat nearly out of my chest. I thought they were coming to get me. *(Shudders)* And then ... then this morning when they did come to get me, I couldn't stand up I was shaking so. My knees wobbled, my stomach churned. And then that guard said, "You, Barabbas! Out! You're free! Get outta here — and don't let us catch you again, 'cause you won't get away the next time." I ... I didn't believe him. I just stood there, shaking. So he gave me quite a jab with his spear and I took off like a bolt of lightning. Then when I got outside I saw the crowd and the commotion at Pilate's and got the word from a bystander that the carpenter was to die in my place — 'cause that's what the crowd wanted.

Joseph: You have been blessed by the Lord, Barabbas.

Barabbas: Yeah, yeah. Lucky, man, just plain lucky …

(Stops abruptly as background noise stops.)

Narrator: "Today you will be with me in paradise."

(Background noise of crowd resumes.)

Barabbas: The noise stopped and started once more.

Joseph: I wonder what's happening up there. I … I'd like to go … but I just can't make myself watch that. It makes me sick to see him cut down like that — and for you, you who don't even appreciate getting off completely free while he dies where you should have died.

Barabbas: All right, all right. So I appreciate it. But, I tell you, it's still just plain luck.

Joseph: *(With finality)* Let's not argue that point any more, Barabbas.

Barabbas: *(With a hearty laugh)* So be it, Joseph.

Joseph: *(Looks toward Calvary again, shakes his head, turns back to Barabbas)* I … I … just can't get over it. Me, a man considered by all who know me to have integrity and honesty as much as any other man around … and I don't have the guts to say, "That man is the Messiah. Don't execute him!" *(Shakes his head again)* I … I just can't get over it. I've got to … got to do … something …

(Background noise of crowd stops.)

Narrator: "It is finished."

(Background noise of crowd resumes.)

Barabbas: Like what, man? Like, if you ask me, I'd just forget about it and get on with my business. From what I've heard … and it's just a little bit since I got released today … from what I've heard, they're going to be after anyone who is on that carpenter's side. I'd just play it cool and safe if I was you.

(Background noise of crowd stops.)

Narrator: "Father, into your hands I give my spirit."

(Distant sound of thunder and rain, rather softly.)

Joseph: No … no … I can't do that. He … he means too much to me. I've got to do something.

Barabbas: Say, listen to that. A thunderstorm! And it's getting dark.

(Lights are dimmed slightly.)

Barabbas: We … we'd better get under cover. But *(Facetiously)* tell me, man, what is it that you're going to do?

Joseph: I … I'm getting an idea.

(Lights are dimmed further.)

(Sound of thunder, rain, lightning cracking gets louder.)

Joseph: I … I'm going to Pilate and offer to take the Master's body … and I'm going to put it in the tomb I've got cut for myself in stone in my garden … over there. *(Points stage left)* Yes, that's it. I'm going to do that. That's the least I can do … whatever the risk.

Barabbas: Well, at least that will save the body from being thrown out on the garbage dump, like they usually do. *(Suddenly shudders)* My God, that's what would have happened to me!

Joseph: You see, Barabbas, you did get saved from quite an end.

(Lights are dimmed further.)

(Sound of storm gets louder.)

Barabbas: *(Looking around, frightened)* If … if this isn't the end of all of us. Look at this darkness … and that storm is fierce … and it's only midday. Let's … get out of here.

Joseph: Just a minute, Barabbas. I told you what I'm going to do. But, what about you? What are you going to do?

Barabbas: Me? I … I don't know. After all, *(Laughs)* I wasn't exactly planning a future after today. I … I didn't expect to be out and around … free again.

Joseph: You'd better think carefully what you will do, Barabbas. *(Pause. Then deliberately)* You know, Barabbas, he died … for … you … so that you could be … be free.

Barabbas: *(Stunned, quizzically)* Yeah … yeah … he … died … for … me. *(Looks around again, in fear of storm)*

(Storm noise gets louder so that characters must shout if necessary.)

Joseph: I … I must go to Pilate. Go, Barabbas, and remember what I've just told you. *(Begins to exit stage left)*

(Lights totally darkened.)

(Storm at intense ferocity. Lightning flashes may be added for effect, through projection or flashing bright spotlight.)

Barabbas: *(Stage center, yelling over storm)* Yeah … Joseph … I'll remember … he … died … for … me … But, I … I don't quite understand that.

6
Pilate and Jesus' Mother After The Crucifixion

The Setting

An armchair, preferably leather, at stage center is only property required. Chair is to be raised one step level above stage floor. If performed in a chancel, the chancel-sanctuary levels may be utilized for this so that Mary is always one step below Pilate.

Costumes

Mary — blue, flowing robe, including veil to cover hair. No makeup or jewelry. Sandals.

Pilate — white toga: long, gold shoulder throw-over, to drag slightly on floor, tied around waist by cord. Elaborate rings on both hands. Laurel wreath (or ivy) ringing top of head.

Directions

Pilate enters slowly, sinks exhaustedly into chair, stares fixedly over heads of audience for some seconds. During opening soliloquy, Pilate alternately paces and sits. He reacts in the same nervous way all during the scene. (See last page for alternate beginning.)

Pilate: What a day! That man … those sniveling Jews … and Caiaphas! Never have I had a day like this one … not even in this forsaken hole. Advice all over the place … release him … crucify him … and he won't say one lousy word. Then, Claudia: "Have nothing to do with this just man." *(Loud "humph")* As if I could ignore him and the whole miserable matter. But, I sure wish I could have. *(Pause)* What a nightmare this day has been! *(Pause)* I wonder … I wonder what it will lead to. *(Pause, shakes head as he resumes)* Nothing … of course … nothing … I'm building it up too much in my mind because there was so much commotion over it. It's all so recent. It's nothing, really, just another commoner executed … amusingly enough, by his own countrymen who bellowed for his death. I've never seen them so worked up at their Festival before. *(Slow, crafty smile)* Gotta hand it to that crafty old Caiaphas and his boys. A real snow job. And it was so obvious. That mob couldn't have cared less, most of them, until Caiaphas and his boys got them all stirred up. *(Pause)* And then that wild storm and earthquake — it just came up out of nowhere — and the darkness. That's the worst I can remember, even here. We've got a job ahead just getting the debris cleaned up. More messes! How, in the name of the gods of Olympus, did I ever get here? Why couldn't I have gotten a plush job in a decent province? Judea! Ugh! The end of the earth! What a nightmare this place is with all their religious nonsense … especially today. *(Pause)* There have been so many others crucified … but there's something just not … just not normal about this one. *(Pause)* Oh, well, I can't spend my time worrying about their damned religious problems. I did wash my hands of that greasy rabbi … and now that I've released his body for burial, I'm through with the whole mess … *(Stops abruptly. Looks to stage entrance.)* Who wants to see me, centurion? *(Pause)* Mary? Mary who? *(Pause)* Never heard of her! How do such people get by the guards? *(Pause)* Oh! *His* mother, eh? *(To himself)* I … I should send her on her way … after all, I'm through with that mess … but … somehow I've got to see her. I'm curious … that's all … just curious. *(To unseen guard)* Very well, send her in, centurion. *(Pilate seats himself, sitting upright and affecting a regal manner.)*

Mary enters, curtseys before Pilate.

Pilate: You have my … my condolences, woman. What is it you want to see me for?

Mary stands, shaking and sobbing. She stands and just stares at Pilate for 10-15 seconds. Pilate grows increasingly nervous.

Pilate: *(Gently, but nervously)* I realize, woman, your … grief. You have, as I said, my condolences … But, you have come to see me … obviously for something … everyone does … so what is it you want?

Mary trembles more, stares at Pilate for another 5-10 seconds.

Pilate: *(Flustered)* Can you not speak, woman? You're as maddening as your … as your son was. *(Forcing himself to be gentle and composed)* I have asked, and I will ask only once more … what is it that you want?

Mary, still trembling, stares a few seconds more. Then, suddenly, in an outburst of angered frustration and grief:

Mary: Why have you murdered my son? What gives you the right to take his life? What has he done? You saw that he was innocent! Yet, you cut off his life at its peak. He was so young … and so important to so many people. *(Waves arms at Pilate)* You … you're a murderer of the innocent. *(Sobs uncontrollably)* My son … my son … my son … *(Falls to knees, continues sobbing.)*

Pilate watches her for a moment, showing anger first, then pity, then slowly returns to controlled regality. Mary slowly controls herself, rises slowly, and addresses Pilate directly.

Mary: Pardon me, sir. I … I did not come here to … to lose my composure like that. But … I … I … oh, my son … *(Bitterly)* Well, were you there when they crucified him? Have you ever seen a crucifixion? The crucifixion of your own son? Those nails … the thud was unbearable … one, then two, then three times. Their thuds will ring through time and eternity. And his arms and feet bled from those ropes. Then … then at the … at the end … when it was … when it was all … *(Sighs)* all over … and that soldier thrust a spear into his side … and the blood spurted out. *(Shudders)* How could you do it? Especially to him?

Pilate: *(Both angry and shaken)* Madam, I am not accustomed to interviewing the survivors of those who have been executed. I grant you an audience … though the gods know not why … and when I do, you proceed to describe a crucifixion to me. I am quite familiar with one. It is, indeed, an ugly, although necessary, process.

Mary: Ugly process? How nonchalantly you say that! You could not care less. It's more than ugly. It's inhumane.

Pilate: *(Irritated)* All right, so it's inhumane. Call it what you will, but stop wasting my time with your opinions. *(Brief pause)* You may go if you have accomplished your business.

Mary: My lord Pilate, forgive my … my outburst. I … I really came here to point out to you … what you have done today.

Pilate: *(Quite irritated)* Woman, I am fully aware of what I have done today, thank you!

Mary: You … you've done more than you realize … you've done more than … than crucify … *my* son.

Pilate: Has your memory died in your grief? Remember that I tried to save him. But your … your petty priests made certain that he it was who went to the cross instead of Barabbas.

Mary: You could have saved him, sir.

Pilate: I? I? Come, woman. You are aware, I presume, that I turned his fate over to your own people. Did you not see me wash my hands? I told the entire crowd … "I am innocent of this man's blood." It's your … your priests' doing that your son got the cross, not mine.

Mary: But, you cannot wash your hands of him, sir. You had the power to say "No" to the crowd. You have dealt with my son … and you have branded yourself … and your future …

Pilate: Watch your tongue, woman.

Mary: Pardon, sir. But, may I ask a question? *(Pilate nods)* How much do you know about my son?

Pilate: I know that he has caused quite a stir among your people … a stir that seemed as if it was going to lead to big trouble for this whole country.

Mary: Do you know much else about his life? About his birth?

Pilate: So he was born. That strikes a common note with all the rest of us … high or low, I might add. We're all the result of man's lust.

Mary: Not my son. He is different. He was conceived before my fiancé and I were married.

Pilate: *(Delighted)* Don't tell me your troubles of the past.

Mary: I had known no man, though, your Excellency.

Pilate: *(Angry)* And don't take me for a fool, woman!

Mary: I am telling you truth, sir. I had known no man. An angel of the Lord God appeared to me. He told me that I could conceive and bear a son, and that I should call him "Jesus." I … I was scared … frightened … because I was a virgin. I didn't know what Joseph would think or do. But, the angel told me that this child would be of God and that he would be holy, conceived of God's Spirit. And then … it happened just as the angel said. I was pregnant.

Pilate: *(Smirking)* And … and what did your fiancé … what was his name?

Mary: Joseph.

Pilate: What did Joseph think of that preposterous story?

Mary: At first, he was quite upset. Then an angel appeared to Joseph in a dream and confirmed what he had told me. From then on Joseph and I have witnessed to this truth. *(Pause)* Then, my son's quite unusual birth … *(Pauses. Looks away, dreamily reminiscing)*

Pilate: *(Edgy, nervous as he notes her total belief in what she has just said)* I … I suppose you're going to tell me that was different, too?

Mary: Yes, sir. Because we had to travel from Nazareth to Bethlehem for the census, Jesus was born in a rough stable there. *(Smiles)* The inns were all overcrowded. Shortly after he was born, a whole angel chorus sang, "Glory to God in the highest" and a bright star brought an almost frightening light to the midnight sky.

Pilate: *(To himself, looking over Mary directly at audience)* A bright light at midnight when he was born … and a midnight darkness at noon when he dies. *(Shudders)* Coincidence? Yes, surely. There must be a scientific explanation. *(Brief pause)* Or else … or else the gods are up to something.

Mary: *(Continues as if uninterrupted)* And then the shepherds on the nearby hillsides came from their work to see him. The shepherds said that the angel in the heavens had called my son "Savior." Before we left Bethlehem, some Eastern kings came to bring my baby gifts. Then we had to go into hiding in Egypt, because Herod was set on killing all the Jewish males under two years old. He had heard that a king had been born … and I guess he was afraid for his power.

Pilate: Ummm … yes … yes … I recall hearing about that … uh … problem. *(Pause)* Go on with your … your incredible and quite amusing story. Most imaginative, woman!

Mary: There are so many, many things. He was so different from other boys through his growing years. I won't bore you with the details of his growing up. It was clear, though, that he was marked by the Lord God for … for … *(Sobs)* … for something special. But, it's been these last three years that have been most important.

Pilate: Maybe so … but I'd say that these last three years have just been cancelled out.

Mary: Cancelled out? No, governor. I don't think that you can cancel out what he has done.

Pilate: *(Angrily) I* have cancelled out nothing, madam. Remember … remember carefully … I washed my hands of your son. Your own people did the cancelling out.

Mary: Have you not heard of what he has done and what he has taught?

Pilate: I have heard only that he was a rabble-rouser … a troublemaker. He has caused one continual stir in this city ever since he came prancing in on that ridiculous donkey last Sunday. Oh, yes, I heard about that … and about upsetting the money-changers' tables in your Temple on Monday. I'd love to have seen that one! Those thieves got what they jolly well deserved. *(Pause)* At any rate, I have indeed heard about your son, woman; he was quite a pest around here this week.

Mary: He was, as you say, "a pest," my lord Pilate, only because he *is* so different.

Pilate: *Was* different, woman. He's … he's dead now.

Mary: I prefer "is," sir. For what he has done and taught will not die. He has taught love … love as helping everyone, even your enemy.

Pilate: No wonder those shrewd priests wanted to get rid of him. They obviously don't love Rome, and they're not about to try either, I'll wager. Of course, we might have used him successfully, if he'd been willing to cooperate with us. Rome would have been most happy had he been able to convince your people to love us ... or even just to be decent to us. After all, we do provide a lot of good things for your ... uh ... backward country.

Mary: *(Undaunted by Pilate's switching the subject)* My son has special power from the Lord God, sir. I myself saw him turn water into wine with but a word. He has instantly healed many who were sick or maimed in body or mind.

Pilate: Your people are always imagining that someone does such things! Poppycock. You're just unrealistic.

Mary: His work is for real, for his power is from God.

Pilate: Come, woman! You people and your God. The gods don't care much about us mortals. *(Pauses)* Oh, well, it has been an interesting, and most unusual story which you have told. Surely a figment of your imagination in your so recent ... uh ... grief. But, woman, I am weary, and the day is almost over. The whole business is done ... over with and done ... your priests saw to that this morning. And I still don't know what it is that you want of me tonight.

Mary: Pardon, sir, but I am now just getting to the point for which I really came to see you. I thought you needed that background information first, though.

Pilate: *(Yawns, appearing bored, tired)* Well, get on with it, then.

Mary: I ... I do not believe that you have heard the last from my son.

Pilate: *(Shudders in fear and anger)* He's dead, woman ... d ... e ... a ... d ... dead ... dead ... and buried ... in a securely locked and heavily guarded rock tomb. I gave those orders myself. That's the end of him. That is the end of your ... your son, woman ... the end of your "king" born without a father. *(Laughs)* Why, come to think of it I wrote that over his cross myself: "King of the Jews."

Mary: I am a poor and simple peasant woman, sir. But, my life's experiences have been most unusual. The Lord God has always done what he has told me he would do. I ... I cannot explain myself very well ... and I'm not sure exactly what I'd say, anyway. But, I ... I just know that none of us has heard the last from him, including you, sir.

Pilate: Watch your tongue, woman ... and remember ... I washed my hands of him. *(Pause)* Anyway, what can a dead man do?

Mary: You could have saved him, sir. Yet, you did not. I think ... I feel ... that what you did ... letting the crowd take over your power and kill my son on a cross ... what you did ... your part in it was all somehow the plan of the Lord God.

Pilate: *(Mocking)* Surely, woman, if all your fantastic stories are true ... as you seem to believe they are ... then this son of yours ... a man conceived by ... by what, did you say? ... the spirit of God ... and born of a virgin ... this half-breed whatever he was would have been saved from death by your apparently incompetent god.

Mary: *(Calmly)* Somehow, sir, my son's death is a part of the plan of the Lord. I ... I *(Sobs)* I'm trying to accept it that way. I cannot explain it. I'm not sure that I fully understand it ... yet. But, somehow, somehow it is part of the Lord's special plan for him ... and you, sir, because you had a part in it, have not heard the last of my son.

Pilate: I determine what I do, woman. Your … your God puts me in no plans of his. Fancy him using a Roman subject in his plans.

Mary: *(Calmly and convincingly)* Somehow, yes somehow, you are in the Lord's plans … and so is my son's death and burial. I believe that the Lord God purposely did not save him this afternoon. I believe … yes … I believe that my son could have saved himself, but that, in obedience to the Lord God's plan, he went to that cross and stayed there to … *(Sobs)* to die. His birth, his healing, his teaching, his suffering today … *(Brief pause as if suddenly enlightened … continues more rapidly)* yes, his suffering … is in the Lord's plan … He suffered under you, Pontius Pilate.

Pilate: *(Disarmed, taken aback)* I … I had nothing to do with his suffering or his death. Your people …

Mary: *(Interrupts)* Yes, he suffered under you, Pontius Pilate, then he was crucified …

Pilate: By … his own people …

Mary: He was crucified; he died *(Slight sob and shudder)* and he has been buried …

Pilate: And that's it, woman! It is done!

Mary: No, my lord Pilate, that is not it. It is not done. I believe that we will yet hear from him again. There is to be something more. I … I don't know what that something more is … but there will be something more.

Pilate: *(Angry and frightened)* Nonsense! Nonsense! He's dead. It's done!

Mary: I have taken enough of your time, sir. I … I wanted you to know that … as hard as this is for me … even as upset as I was when I entered … I … I do not hold my son's death against you.

He himself said, from that … that *(Shudders)* cross, "Father, forgive them, for they know not what they do." *(Pause)* You didn't know, I am sure of that now. *(Pause)* But, this is it … for some reason in the Lord God's plan, my son has suffered under you, under your jurisdiction. He suffered under Rome and under his own … his own people … But, you have the final power over his fate, and so he truly suffered under you, Pontius Pilate. *(Very brief pause)* Good-day, sir; I must prepare for the Sabbath. *(Exits slowly and with great dignity)*

Pilate: *(Sits. Stares)* "Suffered under Pontius Pilate." *(Shudders)* It doesn't all add up … and yet it does … I have the feeling that this day's bloody mess is not over yet … in Rome as well as in Jerusalem … but I couldn't admit that to her. *(Pause)* Fool woman, coming here and upsetting me like this. *(Pause)* "Suffered under Pontius Pilate." *(Pause)* I have the feeling that I haven't heard the end of that one yet, either … that … that I might hear it haunting me for endless years … "Suffered under Pontius Pilate." *(Pause)* A nightmare … a nightmarish, wearying day. *(Yawns)* I must get some sleep … if I can sleep tonight … if I can ever sleep again after all this … "Suffered under Pontius Pilate." *(Pause. Pilate then exits quietly.)*

Alternate Opening

After Pilate enters, while he is sitting in chair staring over heads of audience, solo voice (preferably unseen) sings the spiritual "Were You There?" using only the verse: "Were you there when they crucified my Lord?" At conclusion of music, following a brief pause, Pilate begins opening soliloquy.

Alternate Ending

If the alternate opening was used, same solo voice sings "Were you there when he rose up from the tomb?" from "Were You There?"

OR

If alternate opening was not used, solo voice sings any two verses from the spiritual. Selection of verses for beginning and/or ending can determine whether tone of drama ends with Good Friday or anticipates Easter.

Musical Suggestion

Any verse or verses sung from the spiritual should be sung *a cappella* for greater dramatic effect.